Pirates

Jane Penrose

Contents

OXFORD

UNIVERSITY PRESS

D0586797

What is a pirate?

Think of a pirate. What do you see? A wooden leg? A black hat? An eye-patch? On this page are some famous pirates from films and books. How many of these pirates do you know?

This is Captain Jack Sparrow from the *Pirates of the Caribbean* films. The captain is played by the actor Johnny Depp.

This is Captain Hook from the story *Peter Pan* written by J M Barrie.

Long John Silver is the pirate from the story *Treasure Island*.
The story was written by Robert Louis Stevenson over 100 years ago.

Pirates are a popular subject for stories –
they make great baddies! But did you know
that there are real pirates too? Even today?

Real pirates

Real pirates have been around for thousands of years. They are the thieves of the seas. Some pirates, such as the Vikings, attacked on land as well as at sea.

Viking pirates

Pirates are not just in stories or in the past. This table shows the number of pirate attacks in the Atlantic, Indian and Pacific Oceans from January to May 2007.

Which ocean is the most dangerous for modern pirate attacks?

Number of pirate attacks

Month	Atlantic Ocean	Indian Ocean	Pacific Ocean
January 2007	3	7	1
February 2007	4	7	0
March 2007	3	11	0
April 2007	4	22	0
May 2007	10	27	3

Modern-day pirates attack 'easy' targets like the small **cargo** boat in this picture. Many pirates attack boats to steal money from the **crew** members. Others steal the cargo from the boats they attack.

Pirate treasure

Pirates in stories and real pirates have one thing in common: STEALING TREASURE! For pirates, treasure was anything that was worth lots of money. This didn't just mean gold and silver.

salt

cocoa

gold and jewels

spices

Merchant ships carried things like salt, cocoa, linen and spices. These were worth stealing. Pirates would **plunder** the merchant ships and sell the goods to make money.

It was a rule on board pirate ships that all **booty** had to be shared. The captain got the most!

linen

The story *Treasure Island* is about a pirate who buried his treasure. He made a map to help him find it again. Where do you think the treasure is on this map?

Famous pirates

About 300 years ago there were lots of pirates. Some pirates became very famous. Have you heard of these famous pirates from that time?

WANTED
Henry Every

For attacking a rich Arab ship and stealing its treasure. Nicknames: John Avery, Long Ben and Benjamin Bridgeman.

DISAPPEARED

WANTED
Edward Teach

For stealing lots of treasure and killing or marooning his victims. Nickname: Blackbeard

KILLED IN BATTLE

WANTED
Bartholomew Roberts

For capturing
over 400 ships!
Nicknames: Black Bart,
The Great Pirate Roberts

**KILLED IN
BATTLE**

WANTED
Anne Bonny & Mary Read

For serving in Captain Jack
Rackham's pirate crew,
dressed as men.
Nicknames: Anne Cormac
and Mark Read

PUT IN PRISON

These pirates attacked merchant ships in the seas around Africa, the Caribbean and Europe. They stole precious loads of cocoa, sugar, silver and pearls. They made sailing the seas very dangerous.

On board a pirate ship

Blackbeard was a very famous pirate. His pirate ship was called *The Queen Anne's Revenge*. He stole it from the French. It was one of the most powerful ships of its time.

Toilets
Known as the 'heads', these were holes that went straight into the sea. Watch out below!

Anchor
This was thrown down to the sea floor to keep the ship still.

Crow's nest
(lookout)

Blackbeard's flag

Mast

Guns
Blackbeard's ship had 40 cannons.

Ballast
Heavy stones or other items weighed the ship down to stop it tipping over.

11

Inside a pirate ship

Deck

Galley (kitchen)

Food store
A favourite place for rats!

Captain's cabin
Where the captain would eat, sleep and look at the map.

Powder room
The gunpowder was kept dry here.

Crew's quarters
In some ships, up to 300 men slept here squashed into **hammocks**. It would have smelled terrible!

Captain or powder monkey?

There were lots of jobs to do on board pirate ships.
Some of them were not very nice!
Which job would you prefer?

Captain
Jobs:
- Being a brave leader
- Finding ships to plunder
- Bossing everyone around.

Quartermaster
Jobs:
- Helping with **navigation**
- Punishing pirate rule-breakers
- Giving out food and clothing.

Master gunner

Jobs:
- Making sure the cannons work
- Keeping gunpowder dry
- Stopping cannonballs going rusty.

Powder monkey

Jobs:
- Fetching powder and cannonballs during battles
- Climbing the mast to fix the sails
- Mopping and cleaning – dirty work!

Cook

Jobs:
- Making food for the crew
- Watering down the stew to make it go further
- Keeping rats out of the food store.

Turtles and hardtack

Pirates lived at sea for months at a time. There were no shops and no fridges!

MILD SPICE
For meat that's nearly fresh

MEDIUM SPICE
For meat that's a bit rotten

HOT SPICE
For really old meat

Spices
The cook used spices to hide the taste of rotten meat.

Hardtack
Sometimes the only food was hardtack – tough, dry biscuits. These were often full of maggots so the pirates ate them without looking too closely!

Fish
Fish was kept in salt to stop it going bad.

Live animals
Pirate ships carried live animals so the pirates had fresh meat to eat.

Want to try some hardtack?

Recipe

1. Mix 2 cups of flour with 3/4 cup of water.
2. Add 1 tablespoon of vegetable fat and 6 pinches of salt.
3. Bind together to make a dough.
4. Roll out dough to 1 cm thick.
5. Bake the mixture for one hour at 200°C.
6. Cut into squares.

Don't let the maggots get it!

Surrender!

Pirates often captured merchant ships without fighting. The crew of the other ship would be afraid of the pirates and would **surrender**.

Pirate ships sometimes pretended to be friendly by flying a false flag. Merchant ships played tricks, too. They painted cannons on the side of their ships to look more fierce.

Fighting ships would fire cannonballs at each other. Most cannons could fire the heavy balls nearly 1000 metres!

Boarding

Pirates threw **grappling hooks** onto the merchant ship to pull it closer. Then they swung aboard on ropes or over planks. They fought the crew with swords, pistols and daggers. Then they stole the treasure.

Pirate punishments

Pirates had some horrible punishments for their enemies or for rule-breakers.

Flogging

The quartermaster whipped rule-breakers with a nine-rope whip. This was called a cat-o'-nine-tails.

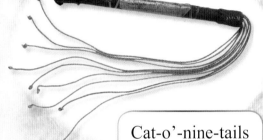

Cat-o'-nine-tails

Keel-hauling

The victim was dragged under the ship from one side to another. They might drown. Or they might die later from cuts from the sharp **barnacles** under the boat.

Barnacles

Tying to the mast

In 1726, one poor cabin-boy was tied to the mast for nine days for stealing. He was also flogged, put in a barrel of seawater and then trodden on by the captain. Ouch!

Marooning

Sometimes pirates who broke the rules were left alone on a deserted island. Their only hope was to be rescued by a passing ship before their food and water ran out!

Captain Jack Sparrow was marooned on an island

21

Pirates on trial

Some pirates were caught by the **navy**. Pirates were bad people and had to be punished.

Some pirates were sold as slaves. They had to work very hard and were treated badly. Many died. Modern-day pirates are put in prison.

Pirates could be locked into a special stand in a marketplace, called a pillory. Passers-by would throw sticks, stones, rotten vegetables and muck at the pirates.

Glossary

barnacle	a small sea creature that fixes itself to the bottom of a boat
booty	stolen treasure
cargo	the goods carried by a ship from one place to another
crew	a group of people who work together on a ship
grappling hook	a metal hook on the end of a rope
hammock	a swinging bed hung between two hooks
merchant ship	a ship that carries goods from one country to sell to another country
navigation	steering the ship the right way
navy	the ships and sailors who help protect a country
plunder	to attack another ship and steal their treasure
surrender	to give up without a fight

Index